8 STEPS AWAY FROM BECOMING A MILLIONAIRE

LANDON GOMES

8 Steps Away From Becoming a Millionaire

Growth Series, Volume 1

Landon Gomes

Published by Landon Gomes, 2023.

8 STEPS AWAY FROM BECOMING A MILLIONAIRE

First edition. August 5, 2023.

ISBN: 979-8223915683

Written by Landon Gomes.

Table of Contents

I dedicate this book to anyone whose been frustrated over the last six - 36 months or generally anyone who felt hopeless and felt like giving up.

My writing this was to help myself and, at the same time help one or two-hundred other individuals who were struggling to find this information.

I meant for this book to be read as a casual conversation and give the reader a play-by-play on how to get the bag. This is for anyone who wants the bag.

Eight Steps Away From Becoming a Millionaire

By Landon Gomes

Introduction: Unlocking Your Path to Financial Freedom

Welcome to an extraordinary voyage of transformation, empowerment, and limitless potential! In these pages, you will embark on an extraordinary quest - one which could take you toward financial independence and the life you've always desired. This book serves not just as words on paper; rather, it acts as your partner and companion on every step along your journey to a financially free existence!

"Am I truly capable of becoming a millionaire?" is often our initial response when confronted by financial goals that seem impossible yet dreams of abundance lie just out of reach. Don't settle for mere fantasy; your goals of financial wealth await your active pursuit.

Start transforming yourself with us - beginning with education and mindset! Understanding money language will open doors of endless potential; with proper tools in your arsenal, you'll discover that many opportunities present themselves to you.

With each chapter, we will explore the secrets to wealth-building success. From job opportunities and personal credit management to starting your own business and using credit for strategic investments - we will arm you with knowledge and strategies for creating multiple streams of income.

But this book goes beyond financial strategies; it offers a whole-life transformation. By viewing life through an abundance lens and asking how every aspect can contribute to growth and prosperity, this work shows you both positive thinking's power as well as how resilience helps overcome difficulties. As you read these pages, you'll witness both concepts at work within yourself.

At Tony Robbins and Les Brown's seminars, you will hear motivational speakers share wisdom that will inspire you to recognize your full potential and trust yourself even when others don't believe. Real-life success stories demonstrate that this journey isn't only for an elite few; anyone willing to step forward and challenge the status quo may join them on this path to self-improvement and happiness.

Each chapter in this guide offers practical steps, with timelines and milestones that enable you to measure progress toward financial independence. As you implement these strategies, your dreams of financial independence will become a reality as you leverage resources, networks, and platforms for business expansion.

This book isn't about instant riches - rather, it demonstrates the strength of perseverance, resourcefulness, and self-belief. As you go through its pages, remember that you deserve this journey and possess all the strength required to see it through successfully.

Are you ready to unlock financial freedom and discover abundance? Your journey awaits; embrace a philosophy-changing mindset, believe in your limitless potential, and let's take steps together to become millionaires - NOW.

Let's embark together on this transformative journey and secure our futures of financial freedom and abundance! Let's make this dream become a reality right now.

Chapter 1 - Education as the Key to Financial Success

Welcome to *Eight Steps Away from Becoming a Millionaire*! In this chapter, we'll examine education's vital role in everyday life and its potential role as an essential contributor toward financial freedom. Additionally, we will delve into different methods of learning available to you — everything from YouTube and Google videos to books to podcasts! So, let's dive right in and discover its transformative potential on our journey toward financial independence!

Understanding the Relationship Between Education and Financial Freedom

Education goes well beyond formal schooling: it is an ongoing journey toward developing knowledge and skills that equip you to make informed decisions. Financial independence hinges on having an in-depth knowledge of money, investing, and entrepreneurship - arm yourself with this information so you can navigate its complexities while making choices aligned with long-term goals.

Education as Empowerment: Unlock Your Potential

Education empowers you to take control of your life and shape its trajectory. There are many educational experiences like traditional school education, workshops, or exploring online resources, and each form of learning holds promise for unlocking your true potential and opening doors of opportunity on the path toward financial freedom. By continuing your pursuit of knowledge, you expand horizons, discover possibilities, and acquire skills necessary for financial independence.

Embracing Technology in Learning Environments

The modern learning landscape has transformed. Thanks to the internet, learning opportunities now lie at our fingertips; from finance tutorials and success stories on YouTube to Google providing answers for any query related to money or wealth-building, access is never far.

Physical and digital books remain timeless sources of wisdom and knowledge, while podcasts provide a platform where experts share insights on various financial subjects. Utilizing technological resources provides endless possibilities to broaden one's horizons while also broadening one's understanding.

Learning From Experts: Seeking Guidance and Mentorship

Along with online resources, engaging with experts and mentors is also key in speeding up your learning journey. Attend workshops, webinars, or seminars led by experienced entrepreneurs or financial gurus, join networking events where like-minded individuals share experiences and offer helpful insight, or attend networking events held by similar businesses to find like-minded peers who form valuable networks of support and share insights among themselves.

Mentors offer invaluable guidance, from providing personalized advice to navigating common pitfalls. Their wealth of experience can serve as both motivation and a source of direction as you work toward meeting your financial goals with certainty and ease.

Never Stop Exploring: Discover Your Curiosity

Curiosity is an invigorating force that drives us all toward growth and expansion. Adopt a curious mindset and never cease seeking knowledge - each day offers plenty of chances to learn something new through TED Talks, documentaries, or finance-related articles. By cultivating curiosity you develop an insatiable thirst for information that keeps your financial journey fresh and engaging!

Balance Learning with Action for Maximum Impact

Education is vital, yet striking a balance between studying and taking action must also be prioritized. Knowledge without application holds little value. Take small steps toward your financial goals proactively as part of your education, taking lessons away with you at each step - whether successful or otherwise! - that will benefit both yourself and society at large.

Conclusion: Encouraging Your Journey

Education is at the foundation of your journey toward financial freedom. Take every opportunity available to you for learning - books, YouTube, podcasts, workshops, or mentorship can all provide great resources - to broaden your horizons and develop sound financial practices which enable you to make sound financial decisions, seize opportunities, and manage challenges successfully.

As you read through this book, remember to harness the power of education and use what you learn for your specific circumstances. Investing more time and energy into yourself means closer achievement of millionaire goals!

Moving forward, let's embark on our next chapter where we explore the exciting world of entrepreneurship and discover its benefits as an avenue towards financial independence. Don't stop being curious, motivated, or learning - your path to becoming a financially empowered individual lies before you!

Chapter 2 - Job: Launch Your Initial Income Funnel

Congratulations on setting yourself on a path toward financial freedom with education! Now it is important that we discuss how crucial finding work, a trade, or a career that meets both personal ambition and market demand will be in achieving financial independence. In this chapter, we cover job search strategies, resume-building techniques, and interview preparation to lay the groundwork for finding meaningful employment to achieve your first source of income.

Craft Your Job Search Strategy

Job hunting can be both thrilling and daunting. To start your job hunt off right, identify your skillset, strengths, passions, and interest areas so that you can narrow down potential job openings that match these characteristics. Use online job portals, company websites, and professional networking platforms like LinkedIn to research available opportunities.

Personalize your resume to emphasize relevant experiences, skills, and achievements that match those required for each position you apply for. An effectively constructed resume significantly increases your odds of landing interviews.

Build Your Resume and Prove Your Value

Your resume is your first opportunity to impress potential employers, so ensure it makes an impression by emphasizing your unique value proposition as well as past accomplishments, skills development initiatives, and any relevant certifications or training that distinguishes you as a professional. Make the first step count: ensure that your resume tells a compelling tale of a professional journey.

Consider providing a personalized cover letter with every job application. A cover letter provides the perfect opportunity to show how excited and qualified you are for the role, as well as show that your skills align perfectly with those needed by the company you're applying to.

Preparing to Succeed: Mastering an Interview

Job interviews provide you with an invaluable opportunity to shine and demonstrate that you are suitable for the position being offered. Conduct extensive research on the company in question in terms of culture, values, and recent accomplishments before crafting thoughtful questions to ask during an interview session that demonstrate a genuine interest in its mission and culture.

Practice common interview questions with a friend or mentor to build communication and confidence, dress professionally, and arrive early for interviews. Maintain an enthusiastic outlook and positive demeanor throughout your interviews - it will leave a positive lasting impression on potential employers!

Finding Meaningful Employment

When it comes to finding any job, focus on aligning it with your long-term career and personal ambitions. Choose an employment option or path that resonates with your values while offering you ample opportunity for skill utilization - purposeful employment can increase job satisfaction while setting you on a path toward future advancement.

Demand in the Market

Demand is of paramount importance in today's job market, so let us examine it by exploring in-demand jobs as an indicator.

As you consider potential job options, take note of market demand for specific roles or trades. Research industries with potential for growth and job openings; target professions that offer long-term viability with career advancement potential. Aligning your skillset with in-demand sectors increases your chance of finding stable yet satisfying employment.

Your Job as a Source of Income

Your job is more than a means to an end; it serves as the initial source of revenue to meet your financial aspirations. Earning from employment provides the foundation for future investments, business ventures, and wealth-building endeavors; therefore, approaching job searches with purpose and intent becomes even more essential.

Conclusion: An Effective Route to Prosperity

Establishing an occupation, trade, or career that aligns with both your ambitions and market demand is the foundation for financial security. Your first source of income will provide stability and set you on your journey into exciting chapters ahead.

In this chapter, we've delved deeper into entrepreneurship and its vast potential. Be true to yourself while applying what you've learned, make timely plans toward reaching your career goals, and take active steps toward them.

Your journey toward becoming a millionaire has only just started, and with thoughtful employment, you are well on your way toward realizing your financial dreams! Take this chapter as an opportunity and apply its strategies with open arms before embarking upon the next chapter in your quest for financial security.

Chapter 3 - Personal Credit Unlocks the Power of Leverage

Welcome to Chapter 3, where we'll delve into personal credit as one of your secondary and tertiary sources of income. It is crucial that we learn about credit scores, reports, responsible management of our personal credit accounts, and proper debt repayment as essential steps toward financial freedom. Here in Chapter 3, we will dive deeper into these essential topics while equipping ourselves with the knowledge, tips, and tricks needed for responsibly using such powerful financial instruments as personal credit.

Learn About Personal Credit and Scores With This eBook

Your credit score is a numerical representation of your creditworthiness, ranging from 300 to 850. It's calculated using several factors like payment history, utilization, and length of history as well as types of loans applied for and new applications submitted. A higher credit score signifies a more reliable borrower, making it easier for you to gain access to financial products with reduced rates as well as possible financial services from reliable providers.

Credit reports provide detailed records of your financial history compiled by credit bureaus. They contain details regarding credit accounts, payment histories, inquiries into your credit profile, and public records such as bankruptcy filings. It's essential that individuals fully comprehend these reports because it directly influences both their score and the terms for various financial products they can acquire.

Building Strong Credit: Tips and Strategies

Are you new to credit or looking to improve it? Don't panic! Successfully building strong credit is a gradual process that takes discipline and responsible financial habits. Here are a few strategies and tips to get you started:

1. Submit Bills Promptly: Make every payment on time as it has an enormously positive effect on your credit rating.

2. Manage Credit Utilization: When managing credit utilization, ensure your balances don't surpass their respective limits as this could have adverse repercussions on your score.

3. Diversify Credit Types: Diversifying your credit types through options such as credit cards, installment loans, and retail accounts can have a beneficial effect on your score.

4. Avoid Excessive Credit Applications: Too many inquiries at one time could negatively impact your score; only apply for credit when necessary.

5. Review Your Credit Reports Regularly: Be vigilant of inaccuracies on your credit reports to ensure accuracy in terms of information displayed about you and dispute any discrepancies to maintain complete accuracy for all parties involved in credit information handling processes.

Responsible Credit Management Is Key to Financial Freedom

Personal credit products like credit cards and lines of credit can be powerful tools for financial leverage; however, you must avoid falling into debt traps. Here are some guidelines for responsible credit management:

1. Avoid Overspending: Make smart use of credit cards and lines of credit to avoid exceeding your ability to repay debt accumulation.

2. Make Additional Credit Card Payments: When possible, try paying more than just the minimum balance due on credit cards to reduce interest charges and speed up debt repayment. Doing this helps accelerate debt relief efforts.

3. Establish an Emergency Fund: Build up an emergency fund in case unexpected expenses arise, decreasing reliance solely on credit when facing financial strain.

4. Remain Informed: It's essential that you remain knowledgeable regarding the terms and conditions of the products that make up your

credit portfolio, from interest rates, fees, and changes that could impact your finances as well as any alterations made that could cause detrimental changes.

5. Credit Limit Management: To avoid maxing out credit cards or using more than 30 - 35% of your available limit, maintain an acceptable utilization ratio to improve the health and performance of your score.

The Trail to Financial Freedom: Managing Credit with Care

Personal credit can help propel you toward financial independence. By building and managing credit products responsibly, creating an established credit profile gives your future endeavors a strong financial platform to thrive on.

Do not view personal credit as free money; rather, it should be seen as an opportunity for financial expansion when used wisely. Take care in using credit products responsibly as these are steps on the journey towards abundance - with discipline, knowledge, and responsibility you are well on your way toward realizing your dreams of prosperity!

Stay focused as we continue our exciting quest toward financial empowerment! In future chapters, we'll cover ways to leverage personal credit to access business lending, acquire assets, and make wise investments. So don't lose focus; let's embark upon this exciting adventure together!

Chapter 4 - Starting Your Own Business and Steps Toward Entrepreneurship

Congratulations on starting on your path to financial freedom! In this chapter, we'll introduce you to the exciting world of starting a business and the opportunities it presents. Launching one is an essential component of realizing your millionaire dreams, so let us guide you step-by-step through every aspect of its formation, from choosing an appropriate business structure to legal requirements and recommended services. Let's embark upon our entrepreneurial adventure together!

Selecting an Appropriate Business Structure

Before diving in headfirst with business registration, let's first explore all available structures and their respective benefits and drawbacks:

1. Sole Proprietorships: Sole proprietorships are one of the easiest forms of business structures to set up and have minimal paperwork requirements. One potential drawback, however, is unlimited personal liability should the business incur debt or legal problems which threaten the personal assets of its owner.

2. Partnership: A partnership exists when two or more individuals collaborate to manage a business together, contributing capital and sharing profits and losses according to a predetermined agreement. Like sole proprietorships, partners also bear personal liability which necessitates having an explicit partnership agreement in place.

3. Limited Liability Company (LLC): LLCs are popular among small business owners due to the personal liability protection they afford their members - meaning personal assets won't be vulnerable against business debts and liabilities. Moreover, an LLC offers flexibility with taxation and management processes, making them attractive options for many entrepreneurs.

4. Corporations (S-corps and C-corps): Corporations are separate legal entities from their owners that offer limited liability protection

to shareholders. S-corps differ significantly from C-corps regarding taxation. S-corps qualify as pass-through entities where profits and losses flow directly back through to individual tax returns while C-corps face double taxation - being taxed both individually as well as corporately.

Each business structure comes with advantages and disadvantages, so choosing the most appropriate option depends on your unique circumstances, long-term goals, and desired level of personal liability protection. When making this key choice it is vital to factor in elements like the number of owners, the nature of business operations, as well as expansion plans.

Guiding You Through Business Registration and Compliance

Now that we understand various business structures better, let's move on to business registration and compliance:

1. Business Name and Structure: Selecting a name and structure for your business are both integral steps in its launch. Your brand identity should be reflected in the name, so make sure it stands out and stands the test of time with potential customers. Ensure your chosen name is memorable without already existing with another business and that any unique trademark registration requirements are satisfied before filing with state/local authorities to legally register it as soon as you've determined an LLC structure (for instance).

2. Obtain Necessary Permits and Licenses: Your business may need specific permits or licenses in order to operate legally, with regulations differing depending on industry and location. It's therefore crucial that you do full research on what permissions and permits may be needed and ensure you obtain them all before taking on new customers or undertaking operations in new places.

3. Employer Identification Number (EIN): An Employer Identification Number is essential for tax filings and official business matters and is issued by the Internal Revenue Service (IRS). You can register your business to get one online through their website.

4. Establish a Business Bank Account: Establishing a separate bank account for your business can help ensure accurate record-keeping and simplified tax filing. Search for banking solutions offering online/mobile/credit card banking features at competitive fees that support effective record keeping.

5. Business Address and Contact Information: Establishing a physical location for your venture adds credibility, especially if it operates from home. You may also consider renting out a virtual office or shared workspace to present an image that remains professional. Furthermore, create dedicated business phone number(s) and email addresses to improve communication between yourself, customers, and suppliers.

6. Compliance With Tax Regulations: Gain familiarity with all relevant taxes applicable to your business structure, including income, sales, and payroll taxes. Keep accurate records of financial transactions while consulting a professional accountant or tax professional as necessary to stay compliant and maximize any deductions available to your organization.

Recommended Services for Establishing a New Business

Establishing a business can be intimidating, but many services exist to make this process less cumbersome:

1. Online Incorporation Services: LegalZoom and Incfile offer convenient and cost-effective business registration services that simplify and expedite registration as an LLC, corporation, or another business entity. These platforms offer time-saving alternatives to managing registration on your own.

2. Business Banking Solutions: Compare offerings from different banks to identify an account that best serves the needs of your business. Search features like online and mobile banking, business credit cards, and low account fees before selecting your favorite account provider. Many financial institutions specialize in business banking packages tailored specifically for startups and small businesses - some may even offer bonuses or fee waivers for newly opened business accounts!

3. Business Insurance Providers: To safeguard your venture against unexpected risks and liabilities, business insurance should be part of your arsenal. Types of policies you should consider include general liability, professional liability, and property coverage, among others. Be sure to visit insurance brokers to assess which coverage best matches the risks your specific venture faces before selecting providers. Compare policies to discover which are most suitable for meeting the requirements of your business needs.

4. Legal Consultation: Work closely with an attorney experienced in business law to cover all legal aspects and tailor your company structure accordingly. Legal professionals can assist in the preparation and review of contracts, agreements, and compliance checks necessary for running your enterprise in accordance with relevant laws and regulations. While cost may be an obstacle for some entrepreneurs, engaging an attorney early may prevent costly legal errors down the road.

5. Accounting and Bookkeeping Services: When it comes to running your own business successfully, managing its finances is absolutely key. Considering hiring professional accounting and bookkeeping services, as that can save time and provide peace of mind that all your records are accurate and organized correctly.

Conclusion: Your Business Dream Takes Off

The successful establishment of your own business marks an impressive step toward financial independence and ensures legal compliance for future success. Congratulations on taking this significant step toward independence!

Starting a business can be both thrilling and daunting; remembering its many obligations require dedication, innovation, and adaptability - so focus on meeting your business goals while treating challenges as opportunities, making entrepreneurship one of the greatest experiences available today!

In the following chapters, we'll explore ways that personal and business credit can help propel entrepreneurial ventures and acquire valuable assets. So, let's move forward confidently knowing that we're well on our way toward financial prosperity through your successful business!

Chapter 5 - Leveraging Personal Credit to Increase Business Loans: Unlocking Opportunities for Growth

Welcome to Chapter 5! Now that you have established strong personal credit and successfully launched your own business, it is time to explore business credit. In this chapter, we'll delve into the process of building business credit compared to personal credit as well as strategies to leverage it for growth and investment opportunities. Prepare to utilize three cash funnels with credit card liquidation opportunities while understanding why having business over personal credit provides significant advantages over time.

Understanding Business Credit and Establishing a Secure Financial Profile

Before delving deeper into how to leverage business credit, it's essential that we establish the difference between personal credit and business credit:

Personal credit refers to your financial history, which encompasses credit cards, loans, and any other obligations tied to personal finances. It's associated with your Social Security number and indicates how well you manage individual credit accounts.

Business credit refers to your organization's financial history and creditworthiness. Once it becomes its own legal entity, an Employer Identification Number (EIN) or Tax Identification Number (TIN) will be given to indicate the creditworthiness of business activities conducted under its authority. Business credit indicates its stability financially as indicated by this number assigned.

Building Business Credit: Steps Toward Financial Reputability

Now that you understand the difference between personal and business credit let's focus on building the latter. Establishing a strong business credit profile is critical to opening various financing opportunities as well as developing credibility within your field of work - here's how to do it:

1. Incorporate Your Business: If necessary, incorporation is the initial step toward creating an independent legal entity and securing an EIN or TIN necessary for building business credit.

2. Open Business Bank Accounts: In addition to opening separate personal and business finance accounts with different bank providers, establish credit relationships with suppliers or vendors who contribute positively towards building your credit history for business use. This helps build it further.

3. Keep an Eye on Your Business Credit Report: Just as with personal credit reports, business credit information can also be reported to credit bureaus. Regularly reviewing this report to check its accuracy and address any discrepancies promptly can help maintain a healthy credit profile and build goodwill among your stakeholders.

4. Build Business Credit with Vendor Credit: As a startup business, one way of building credit quickly is securing vendor credit from suppliers who extend credit terms - whether this means office suppliers, equipment vendors, or industry-specific partners.

5. Apply for a Business Credit Card: Consider applying for a credit card that reports directly to business credit bureaus, using it responsibly while paying all balances promptly to build positive credit histories and create lasting business partnerships.

6. Establish Trade Lines: As your business expands, look for opportunities to establish trade lines with reliable suppliers - these trade lines could include lines of credit or Net-30 payment terms, which contribute positively to building your credit as a company.

7. Progress Toward Business Loans: As your business's credit improves, financial institutions may offer business loans or lines of credit as funding options to aid expansion and investment activities. These financial solutions could prove immensely helpful.

Leveraging Business Credit to Fuel Growth

Once your business credit has been established, leverage it strategically to drive business expansion and seize investment opportunities. Leverage involves borrowing funds to amplify any returns generated through investments; here are several strategies you can employ to successfully leverage it:

1. Establish Business Lines of Credit: Once your business has established an excellent credit history, the next step should be applying for business lines of credit. A line of credit allows access to funds on demand so you can better manage cash flow and seize opportunities for growth.

2. Expansion Strategies: Leverage your business credit to invest in expanding product or service offerings, entering new markets, or initiating marketing initiatives - strategic investments can accelerate business expansion while simultaneously increasing profitability.

3. Acquire New Assets: Leveraging business credit can help increase productivity and competitiveness through purchasing essential assets such as equipment upgrades or technology that enhance productivity and competitiveness.

4. Fund Marketing Initiatives: By funding effective marketing initiatives to reach a wider audience and gain new customers you can increase both revenue and business visibility.

5. Expand Your Team: As your business continues to expand, hiring more employees may become necessary. Fortunately, business credit can cover recruitment and training expenses so that a skilled team is in place to support this expansion.

6. Take Advantage of Investment Opportunities: In business, opportunities often present themselves that require immediate access to capital. Leveraging business credit allows you to act swiftly on favorable investments or acquisitions by quickly accessing funds via financing avenues such as short-term loans.

Benefits of Business Credit Over Personal Credit: An Efficient Strategy

While both personal and business credit are valuable financial tools, business credit offers several significant advantages over personal credit:

1. Separating Personal and Business Finances: Building business credit allows you to maintain a clear divide between personal and professional finances. This not only simplifies accounting processes but also shields personal assets from liabilities related to the business.

2. Higher Credit Limits: Business credit cards and lines of credit typically offer higher credit limits compared to personal cards, giving your business more funds available for expenses and investments.

3. Enhancing Business Reputation: An outstanding business credit profile enhances its standing among suppliers, lenders, and potential partners by showing that your organization can fulfill financial commitments responsibly and is capable of meeting debt payments on time.

4. Opportunities for Growth and Investment: With access to business credit, you can take advantage of opportunities for business expansion, strategic investments, and timely response to market demands.

5. Build a Business Legacy: Establishing a positive credit history can create a legacy for your business that may prove invaluable when considering future expansion, acquisitions, or succession planning. A good profile could open doors of growth opportunities as well as future planning for succession needs.

6. Enhanced Cash Flow Management: Business credit can provide your business with extra working capital, helping improve cash flow management and provide stability during periods of difficulty.

Understanding Business Credit Scores: Dun & Bradstreet Paydex Score and Beyond

As with personal credit scores, business credit scores play a crucial role in securing financing and forging lasting business relationships. One such business credit score is the Dun & Bradstreet Paydex Score, which considers your payment history with vendors and suppliers.

Other business credit bureaus such as Experian and Equifax also provide business credit scores based on various criteria, including credit utilization, trade lines, and public records. Monitoring and improving your business credit scores are integral to unlocking favorable loan terms and financing solutions.

Utilize Your Credit to Avail Funding Solutions

One of the key advantages of building an excellent business credit profile is access to various financing products. As your history improves, financial institutions, lenders, and investors will likely offer credit lines, loans, or investment opportunities more readily.

1. Business Credit Cards: These cards provide one of the easiest forms of business funding available today and allow revolving credit that can be used for various business expenses, while responsible use will boost both your credit score and access to higher limits.

2. Business Lines of Credit: A line of credit is an accessible financing solution, providing funds as they're needed up to your predetermined credit limit. It can provide financial flexibility without locking you into one fixed contract term or giving rise to penalties that can make repayment more complicated than anticipated.

3. Limit. A credit limit provides you with the tools to efficiently manage cash flow and respond rapidly to business opportunities or emergencies.

4. Small Business Loans: Many financial institutions provide small business loans tailored specifically for entrepreneurs' needs, which may be used for equipment purchases, expansion costs, and working capital needs, among other expenses related to running their company.

5. Vendor Financing: Some suppliers and vendors provide financing options through vendor financing programs, enabling you to purchase goods on credit terms without draining cash reserves from your cash flow. Taking advantage of vendor financing could provide essential inventory without straining cash reserves too much.

6. Business Credit Lines From Banks: As your business credit improves, banks may extend an unsecured business line of credit to you that will allow your organization access to funds for various uses throughout its existence.

7. Business Credit Loans From Online Lenders: These have become a convenient source of business financing, thanks to streamlined application processes and quick funding availability, which makes these lenders an appealing option for businesses with immediate financing needs.

Strategies to Properly Utilize Business Credit

Business credit can be an indispensable resource, yet its proper usage must not put your organization into debt traps or cause it to overextend itself. Here are some strategies for effective use of credit:

1. Draft a Comprehensive Business Plan: It is crucial that businesses create detailed business plans which outline their goals, projected revenues, and expenses in detail. A well-thought-out business plan will assist with allocating credit funds efficiently toward areas that fit with your company goals and invest in areas that align with them.

2. Manage Cash Flow Effectively: Maintain a clear understanding of your business's cash flow and budget. Examine financial statements periodically while keeping an eye on performance measures to make sure credit obligations can be handled appropriately by your organization.

3. Avoid Maxing Out Credit Lines: Although credit lines offer access to funds, it's crucial not to exceed their maximum limits as doing so could negatively affect both your score and signal financial distress to lenders.

4. Make Timely Payments: As with personal credit, making timely payments is vital for business credit history management. Be sure to pay vendors, suppliers, and credit card balances promptly to establish yourself as a responsible financial manager.

5. Separate Business and Personal Finances: Avoid mixing personal expenses on business credit cards with those related to work - doing

so makes accounting harder while potentially blurring the distinctions between personal and corporate liabilities.

6. Monitor Business Credit Regularly: To stay ahead of your business credit situation, regularly reviewing credit reports from major business credit bureaus can help ensure accuracy and timely action can be taken should any inaccuracies or discrepancies appear in them. You should take immediate measures if any discrepancies exist.

7. Maintain Strong Relationships With Suppliers: Establishing strong relationships with vendors can open doors to better credit terms and trade deals, building trust with them leads to more advantageous financial arrangements, and arrangements with them can yield positive financial dealings that benefit both parties involved.

Evaluating Business Credit Opportunities: Be Choosey

As your business's credit improves, more offers for financing may arise. While it might be tempting to accept every opportunity presented to you, it is crucial that each one is carefully assessed, taking into consideration factors like interest rates, fees, and repayment terms, as well as possible impact on the financial health and its overall impact on your company.

As you consider various business credit options, aim for those that align with your company's growth strategy and financial goals. Carefully examine potential returns on investments, their effect on cash flow, and overall benefits to your organization when selecting business credit options - being selective can position your enterprise for long-term success!

Building Business Credit for Future Success

Building business credit can be an ongoing endeavor that takes time, effort, and proper financial oversight to manage. By following the strategies outlined herein, you can develop an excellent business credit profile that opens doors for financing options, investment prospects, and favorable terms of trade.

Responsible credit use is key to harnessing its full power effectively. Avoid overextending yourself or solely using it for funding operations - instead, use business credit strategically in support of business growth, investment in essential assets, and to take advantage of opportunities that align with your company goals.

As part of your journey toward becoming a millionaire, this next chapter will cover how to leverage business credit and personal credit to acquire multiple assets. Expand your financial horizons while realizing the full potential of your company's creditworthiness!

Chapter 6 - Leveraging Business Credit to Acquire Assets: Generating Wealth Through Strategic Investing Strategies

Welcome to Chapter 6! As we progress on your path toward millionairehood, let's discover the exciting world of asset acquisition through your business credit. In this chapter, we'll delve into various investment options like real estate, e-commerce, and healthcare businesses as we delve deeper into leveraging debt for income-producing assets while understanding assets versus liabilities concepts. Take charge and unlock your credit potential so you can make strategic investments that generate cash flow while building long-term wealth!

Assets vs. Liabilities: The Foundation of Financial Intelligence

Before diving in and considering specific investment opportunities, it's essential to gain an in-depth knowledge of both assets and liabilities:

Assets: Assets are resources or properties with economic value that generate income or appreciate in value over time, providing your finances with extra cash flow while increasing wealth accumulation. Income-producing assets help build financial security by creating cash flow streams and amassing wealth.

Liabilities: Liabilities, on the other hand, refer to debts that require periodic payment in order to remain payable. Unlike assets that generate revenue or expenses, liabilities must be managed successfully to preserve a healthy financial profile and preserve future opportunities.

Financial intelligence means accumulating more income-producing assets while decreasing liabilities; by doing this, long-term wealth accumulation and financial security become possible.

Investment Options for Growing Your Asset Portfolio

Your business credit can serve as an indispensable financial tool, offering numerous investment possibilities to expand your asset portfolio and help make you an instant millionaire. Let's examine some lucrative asset classes which could generate regular cashflow while contributing towards making that journey possible:

1. Real Estate Investments: Real estate has long been considered an effective means of building wealth. Using your business credit, you can acquire rental properties or commercial real estate through crowdfunding platforms. Rental payments provide passive income, while commercial lease payments provide steady returns from renting space to businesses leasing it out.

2. E-commerce Ventures: E-commerce has enabled entrepreneurs to build profitable businesses online using credit. You can start or acquire stores selling popular products that generate sustainable profits with minimal overhead costs and potential scalable income potential.

3. Airbnb and Short-Term Rentals: If you already own property, using business credit to furnish and market it as an Airbnb rental may yield higher returns compared to traditional long-term lease agreements.

4. Infinity Banking/Infinite Banking Concept (IBC): IBC involves creating your own private bank system by using specially tailored whole-life policies as the building blocks. You can then expand using business credit to fund them and access cash value to use for investments while keeping tax advantages.

5. Healthcare Businesses: Investing in healthcare businesses like medical practices or home healthcare services can be enormously satisfying and profitable over time. As this sector remains strong and expanding, investing in it may make an excellent long-term bet.

6. Franchise Opportunities: Franchises provide proven business models. Using business credit to invest in one can enable you to take advantage of an established brand and support structure and increase the odds of profitability.

7. Digital Products and Intellectual Property: Create digital products such as eBooks, online courses, or software and leverage business credit for marketing and distribution to generate passive income with minimal ongoing expenses.

8. Peer-to-Peer Lending: Certain platforms allow investors to utilize their business credit by engaging in peer-to-peer lending - lending money directly to individuals or small businesses via loans - for attractive returns in interest payments. This form of investing could bring substantial returns.

9. Stock Market Investments: While investing in the stock market comes with its own risks, it can also serve to diversify your asset portfolio. You can fund stock purchases using business credit lines or invest in exchange-traded funds (ETFs) and mutual funds.

Strategic Debt Leverage Using OPM

OPM stands for Other People's Money. Strategic debt leveraging involves using OPM-like loans or lines of credit from outside sources to acquire income-producing assets that generate a greater return than what was borrowed. By using your business credit as collateral for these types of borrowing arrangements, your investments could generate greater returns than any associated costs of borrowing money.

OPM allows you to leverage your capital and increase its potential returns by using debt to increase asset acquisition capacity without depending on personal funds alone. But this strategy must be approached carefully; ensure all necessary risk assessments have been performed prior to making investment decisions.

Diversification and Risk Management Strategies to Safeguard Investments

As your asset portfolio expands, diversification becomes essential to risk management. Dividing investments across asset classes reduces overall exposure; should one investment underperform, others can offset any potential losses and help ensure overall financial security.

Effective Risk Mitigation and Diversification

1. Undergo Exhaustive Research and Due Diligence: Prior to investing, thoroughly investigate and research each asset's potential risks and rewards by considering factors like market trends, competition, regulatory considerations, etc.

2. Alternating Between Short and Long-Term Investments: Strive to create a portfolio composed of both short-term and long-term investments. Short-term investments provide liquidity with quick returns while long-term investments may provide sustainable income and appreciation over time.

3. Stay Informed and Adapt: As financial landscapes continue to shift, remain informed on market trends and economic indicators while being ready to adjust your investment strategies as required.

4. Rely on Professional Advice: For improved insight and informed decisions, seek professional financial advisors or investment specialists' assistance in making wise financial choices tailored specifically to your financial goals and risk preferences. Professional guidance can provide invaluable insights that help make informed financial decisions that align with personal values and needs.

5. Establish Realistic Goals: Set clear financial goals with realistic expectations regarding investments to avoid unrealistic returns or unnecessary risk-taking.

6. Build Assets, but Also Establish Emergency Funds: While building assets is of course essential, don't overlook the importance of creating and keeping emergency funds as part of an asset-building strategy. Having ready funds available could provide much-needed protection in times of sudden financial difficulty.

Embracing Entrepreneurial Spirit for Continuous Learning and Growth

As you venture into asset acquisition and investment, embrace an entrepreneurial mindset of continuous learning and growth. The investment landscape can change quickly over time; therefore, adaptability is necessary when exploring potential new investments.

Investing in yourself through education, skill acquisition, and networking is equally essential to reaching financial success. Seek guidance and assistance from people who share similar financial objectives and who can provide essential support and insights.

Building Wealth Legacy Through Inheritance

Congratulations on reaching a critical stage on your path toward becoming a millionaire! Utilizing business credit, strategic debt, and OPM as tools have opened the door to income-producing assets which could provide long-term wealth over generations, resulting in your legacy of financial security and lasting prosperity.

As you proceed with asset acquisition, remember to exercise careful planning, diversification, and risk management. Make use of business credit wisely while aligning investments to your financial goals and tolerance for risk.

In the next chapter, we'll investigate the importance of creating multiple streams of income and how they can accelerate your journey toward financial freedom. Prepare yourself to expand your wealth-building strategy and explore all its possibilities!

Chapter 7 - Money Creation: Scaling Your Business and Generating Abundance

Welcome to Chapter 7, where we'll delve deeper into money creation through product and service development and business expansion. By now, you have garnered considerable knowledge on both personal and business finances, created multiple streams of income, and leveraged business credit effectively for strategic investments. Time to step up your entrepreneurial game! Offering valuable products and services that meet market requirements will propel exponential business expansion. In this chapter, we'll reveal the secrets to successful money creation - from encouraging innovation to hiring an ideal team that adds value and strengthens your business. Get ready to unleash the full power of your entrepreneurial spirit and experience abundance both physically and financially!

Fostering Innovation for Successful Product and Service Development

As an aspiring millionaire, your ability to create value in the marketplace is of vital importance. Innovation plays a central role in the creation of products and services that resonate with target audiences. Here are a few steps for cultivating innovation to bring products or services that satisfy this goal:

1. Conduct Market Research to Pinpoint Needs and Pain Points in Your Target Market: Conducting market research in order to pinpoint unmet needs and pain points within your target market helps you gain an understanding of customers' desires, challenges, and preferences so as to guide product and service development efforts effectively.

2. Bring New Ideas Forward: To encourage creative and out-of-the-box thinking within your team, brainstorm new products and services that meet market requirements while expanding upon what

already exists in terms of market demand and complementing current offerings.

3. Prototype and Test: Create prototypes or minimum viable products (MVPs) to assess feasibility and appeal, solicit feedback from potential customers to inform your offerings, and take necessary actions based on this feedback to optimize and hone them further.

4. Continuous Improvement: Adopt a culture of continuous improvement within your organization by actively seeking feedback, monitoring market trends, and adapting products/services accordingly.

5. Invest in R&D: Allocate resources towards research and development (R&D), so your products have an edge against competitors. This could involve looking into emerging technologies, trends, and innovations - allocating funds toward these areas can give you a competitive advantage!

6. Create an Intact Brand Identity: Branding plays a pivotal role in product and service creation, so establish one with values that resonate with your target market.

7. Deliver an Outstanding Customer Experience: Concentrate on providing extraordinary customer experiences to maximize brand advocacy. Delighted customers can become strong long-term backers of your brand.

Scaling Your Business: Unlocking Exponential Growth

Scaling your business means expanding operations and resources in response to increased customer demands and helps achieve exponential expansion. Here are some effective strategies for scaling your enterprise:

1. Optimize Operations: Improve efficiency and productivity within your business processes to boost efficiencies and cut redundancies to prepare for growth. Identify bottlenecks to eliminate possible redundancies to prepare yourself for expansion.

2. Leverage Technology: By adopting technology to automate tasks, improve communication, and enhance customer experiences you can streamline operations while freeing resources up for growth initiatives.

3. Increase Marketing Efforts: Extend your marketing efforts in order to reach more audiences and acquire new customers by employing digital, social, and content strategies to expand brand visibility and expand your reach.

4. Diversify Income Streams: Seek new opportunities to diversify your income streams. Expanding product lines or venturing into complementary markets can reduce risks while simultaneously increasing profitability.

5. Invest in Talent: To succeed at scaling, your business requires an adept and motivated workforce. Therefore, invest in talent acquisition and retention programs to establish an experienced staff that aligns with your business goals.

6. Establish Partnerships: Looking for new markets, sharing resources, and capitalizing on each other's expertise are just three of the great benefits that partnerships provide businesses.

7. Monitor Financial Health: To keep your business growing successfully, it's critical that its foundation remains financially strong. Assess and review your status regularly while effectively monitoring cash flow and planning for growth opportunities.

Hiring to Expand: Building Value Into Your Company

As your business expands, talent requirements increase accordingly. Hiring talented personnel is integral for adding value and correcting deficiencies within your organization. Here is how you can attract and keep top talent:

1. Establish Roles and Responsibilities: Establish roles and responsibilities for every position within your business to ensure alignment with its strategic goals.

2. Cultivate an Attractive Company Culture: Create an environment that attracts talented employees whom your company values.

3. Provide Competitive Compensation and Benefits: Provide attractive compensation packages and attractive benefits packages in order to attract and retain top talent in the market.

4. Invest in Employee Development: Provide employees with opportunities for professional and personal growth within your organization. Making this investment will foster loyalty while building an experienced, skilled, and productive workforce.

5. Implement Performance-Based Incentives: Utilizing performance-based incentives is one way of rewarding outstanding performances and motivating exceptional employees to excel.

6. Create an Inclusive Workspace: To foster creativity and innovation within your organization, promote diversity and inclusion at work by cultivating diverse and inclusive work environments.

7. Promote Work-Life Balance: Emphasize the importance of work-life balance to support employee well-being and productivity.

Strategic Partnerships to Accelerate Growth and Broaden Market Reach

Strategic partnerships can significantly impact your company's growth and market reach, in addition to recruiting talented employees. Collaborating with other businesses or influencers can open doors and access uncharted markets. Here's how you can form successful strategic alliances:

1. Shared Vision and Goals: When selecting partners, be sure they share similar vision and business goals. A mutual understanding of what the partnership stands for encourages mutual commitment and success in partnership relationships.

2. Complementary Expertise: For optimal success in business and operations, look for partners that bring complementary expertise or resources that will lead to enhanced products or services and streamline operations.

3. Communication and Agreements: Establish clear channels of communication and formal agreements among partners outlining each party's responsibilities, expectations, and contributions.

4. Mutual Benefit: To ensure the partnership will bring value for both parties involved every partner should get something out of it.

5. Assess and Evaluate: Assessing partnerships is vitally important. Be willing to adjust or terminate those that no longer align with your business goals and continue measuring effectiveness over time.

Unleashing Growth Mindset for Continuous Learning

Scaling your business and creating abundance requires adopting a growth mindset; that is, believing you can learn, adapt, and reach higher levels of success. In your journey through money creation and entrepreneurship, embrace these three principles:

1. Continuous Learning: Stay current by attending workshops, seminars, and industry events that address current trends and innovations.

2. Learn From Challenges: Approach obstacles as opportunities to evolve your knowledge. Success on any entrepreneurial journey requires confronting and surmounting them.

3. Be Resilient: Entrepreneurship can present its share of challenges. Stay resilient to reach long-term success and overcome setbacks as you strive to meet goals.

4. Network and Collaborate: Form meaningful connections with fellow entrepreneurs, mentors, and industry experts who share similar goals to you - being supported by like-minded people can propel your success!

5. Always Prioritize Customers' Needs and Preferences: To achieve innovation and sustained growth, always put customers' needs and preferences ahead of your own. A customer-centric approach drives innovation.

Conclusion: Join the Journey of Money Creation

Congratulations on mastering the art of money creation through product and service development as well as expanding your business! You have found your niche.

Chapter 8 - Philosophies on Mindshift Altering for Wealth-Building Success

Welcome to being steps away from becoming a millionaire!" In this final chapter of *Steps Away from Becoming a Millionaire*, we will examine how successful entrepreneurs embrace a growth mindset and cultivate positive attitudes about wealth building - integral components to becoming a millionaire! In addition to discussing positive thinking practices such as overcoming challenges with optimism as well as understanding our own potential and believing in ourselves even when others don't, this chapter also delves deep into unlocking the unlimited potential within yourself, cutting ties with negativity while embarking upon a path of constant expansion. Prepare to unlock and unleash all the boundless potential within yourself while cutting ties with negativity on an unparalleled path toward constant elevation and expansion of growth!

Embracing Positive Thinking to Form a Growth Mindset

At the core of every successful millionaire lies an adaptable growth mindset: believing one's abilities and intelligence can be developed with dedication and hard work. Positive thinking plays an instrumental role in developing this attitude; by cultivating positivity you shift focus away from limitations towards possibilities, thereby opening yourself up to wealth-building success opportunities. Here's how you can harness its power:

1. Recognize Your Potential: Recognize that you possess untapped potential and have the ability to achieve greatness. Adopt an optimistic perspective while challenging self-limiting beliefs which might be restricting your growth and achievements.

2. Visualize Your Success: Visualizing the road to your desired outcomes will assist with making plans to reach them more rapidly.

Visualization enables us to set our actions toward our desired goals more successfully and get closer to achieving them faster.

3. Practice Gratitude It's important to maintain an upbeat mindset and positive outlook on life's blessings as well as on the progress made on your millionaire journey. Cultivating an everyday gratitude practice is vital to maintaining positivity and encourages progress toward wealth accumulation.

4. Surround Yourself with Positivity: Choose to surround yourself with positive influences such as motivational books, podcasts, and mentors that motivate and edify.

5. Utilize Failures as Lessons: View failure and setbacks as opportunities to grow as much as you can and use mistakes made along the way to reach success.

6. Create Realistic Goals: Break your millionaire goals down into actionable steps that are easily manageable, celebrating each milestone as proof of your growth and using this as motivation for further progress.

7. Practice Positive Self-Talk: Substitute negative self-talk for positive affirmations to encourage yourself daily and reinforce your belief in your abilities.

Overcoming Challenges on the Path to Success

Journeying toward millionairedom can be daunting and requires disciplined dedication to remain motivated and resilient during its ups and downs. Here are strategies for staying on course to achieving your success:

1. Accept Change as Part of Growth: Acknowledging change as an inexorable component of growth is vitally important - adaptability will enable you to navigate uncertain waters successfully while also seizing new opportunities that arise.

2. See Setbacks as Learning Experiences: Rather than seeing setbacks as failures, use these experiences as opportunities for self-improvement and progression. Examine what went wrong to gain insights that help move you in the right direction.

3. Seek Support and Mentorship: Surround yourself with mentors, peers, and friends that can offer guidance and comfort during difficult times.

4. Remain Committed to Your Vision: Regularly review your millionaire vision and remember why you started on this journey. Remain committed to reaching your goals even when facing setbacks or being met by obstacles.

5. Engage in Self-Care: Take steps to maintain both physical and mental well-being by practicing regular exercise, mindfulness practices, and restful sleeping patterns - these practices help build your resilience against challenges faced in daily life.

6. Break Down Tasks: When faced with daunting tasks, break them into more manageable steps so they feel less daunting and enable you to face them head-on more confidently

7. Celebrate Small Wins: Celebrate each accomplishment no matter how minor! Acknowledging progress fuels motivation to continue moving in a forward trajectory.

Reasons Why It Is Vital to Believe in Oneself

Becoming a millionaire requires making difficult choices and breaking away from negativity in your life. Only certain individuals may understand and support your journey towards wealth-building success, which is why believing in yourself and your goals even when others doubt them is key. Here is how you can manage this challenging aspect of mindset:

1. Focus on Your Vision: Keep the goal of becoming a millionaire at the forefront of your mind, staying committed to reaching it, while resisting outside influence that would tempt you away from reaching them.

2. Reduce Exposure to Negativity: Be wary of negative influences such as family, friends, and social media that may undermine and bring you down; instead, surround yourself with supportive people who can uphold and uplift you.

3. Seek Like-Minded Communities: Join communities or networking groups that foster growth and positivity to enhance your journey.

4. Protect Your Energy: Be conscious of how negativity negatively impacts both your physical and mental well-being, set boundaries with those who repeatedly undermine you, and set aside any relationships which pose a potential risk to your mindset.

5. Convert Criticism into Motivation: Use criticism and doubt as fuel for motivation, showing yourself and others that you're capable of realizing your dreams.

6. Mark Your Successes: Acknowledging your successes - no matter how small - serves as an indicator of progress and potential. Take pride in each achievement to remember where you have come.

Tony Robbins and Les Brown Provide Empowering Quotes for Mindset Transformation

Motivational speakers and thought leaders throughout history have provided profound advice that has the power to shift mindsets. Take two renowned individuals such as Tony Robbins and Les Brown: they both possess powerful knowledge that could spark transformation within you.

Tony Robbins said it best: "Imagination and commitment are your only limitations in creating change in this world."

As Les Brown said: "If you set goals and pursue them with all your energy and determination, your gifts will take you places you never imagined they could go."

These words serve to remind us that our potential is unlimited and that success requires creativity, determination, and perseverance. Take inspiration from these influential speakers as a foundation for shifting your mindset transformation journey.

Expand Your Reach by Seeking Constant Elevation

As you have explored each chapter, you have gained greater insights into personal and business finances, leveraged credit for investments, and explored different sources of income. Now is the time to embrace continuous elevation as part of an ever-evolving journey of personal and professional growth in all aspects of your life.

Success is not an endpoint but rather a pursuit throughout one's lifetime. Once your first millionaire goals have been reached, continue setting more ambitious ones to expand your potential even further. Keep learning, adapting to change and continually raising yourself up until success has eventually found you! Elevation can unlock many doors to success if pursued diligently enough.

Live a life filled with abundance and fulfillment.

Mindset Transformation Testimonials and Real-Life Success Stories

Real-life success stories provide convincing proof of the power of mindset transformation. Below are a few testimonials from individuals who have harnessed positive thinking and resilience on their paths to wealth-building success:

Testimonial 1 - Emily's Journey to Financial Freedom

"As I was growing up, I never believed in becoming a millionaire. After reading *Steps Away from Becoming a Millionaire*, however, my mindset began holding me back and changed significantly; adopting a growth mindset helped me visualize success more readily; I began investing [in] real estate using business credit; now [I] own multiple rental properties which generate passive income - I know my journey continues but know with positive attitude and determination it can bring even greater financial freedom."

Testimonial 2 - Alex's Story of Overcoming Adversity

"Throughout my journey towards becoming an accomplished entrepreneur, I faced many hurdles. People questioned my abilities and decisions; yet, I stayed committed to my vision without giving in to negativity. Instead, I learned from setbacks, sought mentorship from knowledgeable peers, and created supportive networks of supporters - these efforts enabled me to launch and sustain an e-commerce store and diversify income sources - showing resilience and an ability to pursue growth as my path."

Conclusion: Adopt the Mindset of a Millionaire

Congratulations on reaching the conclusion of *Steps Away from Becoming a Millionaire*! You now possess all the knowledge and tools to transform your life through mindset development and financial empowerment. Remember, though; mindset influences all areas of our lives including beliefs, decisions, and actions taken.

Accept and harness the power of positive thinking and a growth mindset to tackle life's obstacles with resilience and trust yourself even when others don't believe. Avoid negativity by surrounding yourself with like-minded people who uplift and support you; take inspiration from motivational leaders like Tony Robbins or Les Brown on your path toward success!

As you make progress toward wealth-building, keep this in mind: wealth creation doesn't just involve making more money - rather, wealth-building should involve fulfilling and realizing all the potential within yourself and building an exceptional life filled with abundance, fulfillment, and purpose. Adopt the mindset of a millionaire for greater achievements and lasting prosperity!

May your journey be filled with boundless expansion and realization of all your wildest dreams! Adopt an unshakeable philosophy-changing mindset and become the millionaire you have always desired to become! Your future awaits; harness its potential now. Go forth and conquer!

The End

• • • •

Don't stop here ... there's more to go!

Bonus Chapter - Plan of Action to Reach Millionaire Success.

CONGRATULATIONS ON reaching this bonus chapter! You have gained invaluable knowledge regarding personal finances, business strategies, and the mindset needed to become a millionaire. Now it is time to put this knowledge into action on the road toward financial freedom. We will outline step-by-step implementation plans with timelines and milestones as well as provide strategies on leveraging resources such as networks or platforms for growth - let us show you how! It is now up to YOU and only YOU are responsible for realizing your dreams!

Step-by-Step Implementation to Achieve Success

1. Education and Mindset Shift: To start this journey of financial success, begin reading "Chapter 1 - Education as the Key to Financial Success." Get acquainted with money basics while developing a growth-minded attitude toward finances. Take time out for learning through various mediums like books, podcasts, online courses, or seminars.

2. Explore Job Opportunities: Continue on to "Chapter 2 - Job: Launch Your Initial Income Funnel," where you will discover job opportunities that align with your skills and ambitions, create custom resumes to showcase them effectively at interviews, and prepare yourself confidently.

3. Establish Strong Personal Credit: In "Chapter 3 - Personal Credit Unlocks the Power of Leverage," learn all about credit scores and reports. Build and sustain good credit by paying bills on time while managing any outstanding debts responsibly.

4. Starting a Business: "Chapter 4 - Starting Your Own Business and Steps Towards Entrepreneurship," provides guidance on various business entity types and registration. Take steps to set up and register your entity by creating a company website and email account as soon as possible -

you also may require other essential elements like physical addresses for delivery services to function effectively.

5. Utilize Business Credit for Expansion: "Chapter 5 - Leveraging Personal Credit to Increase Business Loans: Unlocking Opportunities for Growth," details how to establish business credit and use this line of credit to acquire income-producing assets.

6. Acquire Cash-Flowing Assets: In "Chapter 6: Leveraging Business Credit to Acquire Assets: Generating Wealth through Strategic Investing Strategies," explore investment possibilities like real estate, e-commerce, and healthcare businesses as ways of creating passive income from assets that you acquire through loans or credit lines. Start investing now in assets that generate passive income!

7. Adopt Positive Thinking and Resilience: "Chapter 7: Money Creation: Scaling Your Business and Generating Abundance" will motivate you to embrace positivity and overcome difficulties by adopting an optimistic viewpoint and resilient character traits. Your mindset lays the groundwork for future success!

8. Break Free From Negativity: Expand on what was discussed in "Chapter 8: Philosophy on Mindshift Altring for Wealth-Building Success," by surrounding yourself with positive influences that support your quest of becoming a millionaire. Join like-minded communities which provide encouragement during this journey.

9. Create an Action Plan: Use the step-by-step guide in this "Bonus Chapter - Plan of Action to Reach Millionaire Success" to achieve your financial goals.

Successful Timelines and Milestones for Tracking Progress

- First Three Months: Complete your education and mindset shift, establish an excellent personal credit score, and begin exploring job opportunities aligned with long-term goals.

- 3 to 6 Months: Establish and register your business entity, such as an LLC, S-corp, or C-corp, and begin building business credit by using personal credit wisely for business.

- 6 to 12 Months: Acquire an income-generating asset such as rental real estate or an online store to build out and diversify your revenue stream. Afterward, work on expanding and scaling up your business operations while diversifying income sources.

At this stage, your portfolio should have begun generating passive income and you should continue investing in real estate as well as exploring other ventures such as healthcare businesses or digital products.

- 3 to 5 Years: Reevaluate progress and revisit financial goals, potentially expanding business operations or exploring new markets or industries for further expansion.

Leveraging Everything: Unleashing Resourcefulness

As you journey toward becoming a millionaire, view everything through a lens of leverage. Ask yourself "How will this serve me in the future?" or "What alternative means can this relationship, job, friendship, school skill, etc. provide to help me achieve financial independence?"

- Leveraging Relationships: Expand your network, cultivate meaningful connections with like-minded individuals, mentors, and potential partners, and use these relationships for mutual growth and support.

- Leveraging Your Skills and Education: Retain and expand your skills through ongoing professional development programs or certifications that add value to your business and open doors to additional income-generation possibilities. Your expertise will enhance your success.

- Utilize Social Media and Platforms: Social media is an ideal platform to leverage for promotion, building brand recognition, and connecting with potential customers. Explore online marketplaces as an avenue for expansion as well as for increasing sales.

- Diversify Your Income Sources: Diversifying your income through investments, passive sources, and side hustles is vital to achieving financial security. Every additional stream contributes toward this end goal.

- Leveraging Time and Effort: Delegate tasks that don't need your direct involvement; focus instead on high-impact activities to drive your business forward and maximize productivity.

Conclusion: Unleash Your Potential and Claim Your Destiny

Assuming you now possess an action plan to become a millionaire, remember success is not a destination; rather, it should be treated as an ongoing journey of constant elevation and expansion. Adopt a growth mindset, overcome any hurdles along the way, and remain committed to your vision. Cut ties with negativity by surrounding yourself with positive people who support your goals.

Track and celebrate every step toward your millionaire dreams using achievable timelines and milestones, using resources, networks, and platforms available to you to take your business or financial success to new heights.

As you venture forth on this journey, remind yourself that this experience is all yours and that anything can be accomplished when you set your mind to it. Adopt an optimistic philosophy-changing outlook, have faith in yourself even when others don't, and claim your destiny as a millionaire! The world awaits your greatness so step forth and leave your mark!

Now is the time to act; your journey towards millionairedom starts now!

An Epilogue on Accepting Your New Reality

Congratulations, dear reader, on reaching the conclusion of *Steps Away From Becoming a Millionaire*! Your journey of self-discovery, financial empowerment, and mindset change has come full circle; now take a moment and reflect upon all that has changed as your dreams now become tangible realities.

These pages have presented you with an in-depth introduction to financial success. Through education and a growth mindset, you have discovered your true potential and charted a path towards wealth creation triumphs. Equipped with this knowledge you have launched ventures, secured multiple streams of income, and established the basis for an abundant life.

But this is more than the end of a book; this marks a new phase in your life! Now equipped with the tools, strategies, and wisdom necessary for reaching financial freedom, we welcome this next phase and offer words of advice and encouragement as you embark upon this exciting new reality.

- Remember Your WHY: As you embark upon this quest, keep the reason you started it close to your heart. Whether your motivation is creating better futures for loved ones, supporting worthwhile causes, or finding personal fulfillment, let this purpose act as the fuel behind your determination and stay true to it throughout this endeavor.

- Celebrate the Journey: Building wealth and reaching success is a journey, not an endpoint. Enjoy each step as it passes and celebrate every achievement as each milestone demonstrates your courage and resilience.

- Ongoing Education: In pursuit of greatness, never stop learning. Be curious, stay open-minded to new concepts, and seek knowledge from diverse sources - this world holds endless potential that is just waiting to be unlocked and explored!

- Get Assistance: Remind yourself that you're not on this journey alone. Reach out for guidance from mentors, peers, friends, and family alike - surround yourself with those who encourage and uphold you on this path to greater financial health and well-being.

- Adapt and Evolve: As our world is forever shifting, so should your strategies. Be ready to adapt as the environment shifts around you; adapting quickly is part of being a successful entrepreneur. Embracing change is something all successful businesspeople understand well.

- Gratitude and Generosity: As you reach success, don't lose sight of the importance of gratitude and generosity when it comes to giving back. Share the fruits of your labors, support others along their paths to fulfillment, and leave an indelible mark in this world!

- Celebrate Yourself: Take time for yourself to commemorate all your successes - big or small. Acknowledge all the hard work, commitment, and effort put forth into reaching your dreams; celebrate who you have become as well as all that lies within.

- Visualization and Manifestation: Keep visualizing your dreams and aspirations, envision yourself living an abundant and successful lifestyle, and then manifest them with unfaltering belief and decisive actions.

- Enter Into Success: With newfound wealth and prosperity comes endless opportunities that you would have never considered previously. You have the power to color this world with colors of abundance and possibility.

As you transition into this new reality, keep the journey in mind: keep pushing past what seems achievable because your potential is infinite! Be open to exploring new ventures, growing existing businesses, and making an impactful contribution that affects others' lives positively.

Never lose sight of what drove this journey: an ever-evolving mindset. Your philosophy shift has enabled you to change your life, embrace abundance, and set out on the journey toward becoming a millionaire.

Are you ready for change, dear reader? Take hold of your future now! Now equipped with knowledge and mindset tools that enable you to reach financial independence, we believe in you! Let the journey commence now!

Now is your opportunity to unleash the millionaire within you and ignite this world with your brilliance! Go forth and blaze a trail.

With the sincerest gratitude and warmest greetings,

Authors of *Steps Away from Becoming a Millionaire*

Acknowledgments

It brings me great pleasure and immense appreciation to write these acknowledgments of those who have touched my life, encouraged my journey towards millionairedom, or simply been there along my journey as mentors, supporters, or motivators along my path towards financial security. Without such remarkable people in my life and surroundings, I could never hope to succeed and achieve such heights - I feel profoundly humbled that success comes so easily for so many!

Honorable Mentions to All the Wonderful YouTubers: Thank you to the YouTubers whose thoughtful videos have provided me with continuous inspiration and knowledge! Your dedication to providing high-value content has enabled me to expand my horizons and embrace new opportunities; your enthusiasm fueled within me my drive for unflinching greatness. I wish you every success in your careers!

To the Social Proof Podcast: Thank you for providing thought-provoking conversations with industry leaders and game changers, offering unique perspectives, innovative strategies, and broadened perspectives that have expanded my knowledge about wealth-building horizons while challenging me to think beyond conventional boundaries. Your podcast has provided immense wisdom. Thank you again.

To Kevin Samuels: Your wisdom, charisma, and relentless pursuit of excellence have left an indelible imprint on my journey. Your empowering messages taught me the significance of self-worth, personal improvement, and setting high standards - thank you for being my guide along this journey to success!

To EYL University: Thank you EYL University for being such an invaluable source of knowledge and resources! Your dedication to financial education has played an instrumental role in my approach and mindset toward wealth accumulation - your platform truly represents transformation!

To Peggy Stamps: Your mentorship and unwavering confidence in my potential have been truly transformative. Thanks for always believing in my abilities despite any fears I might have had and encouraging me to stretch beyond my comfort zone and explore opportunities that seemed out of reach - thank you for always being such a source of strength and guidance!

To My YBI Team: Thank you to my team at YBI for always being there when needed and supporting my endeavors with dedication and teamwork. Your collaborative spirit and tireless efforts have brought my dreams to fruition; thanks to you we've reached milestones that once seemed unobtainable, and each member's contribution makes this achievement all the sweeter for me!

To My Parents: From day one, you have always been there as my unwavering source of love and support. Your belief in me, endless encouragement, and sacrifice have built the basis of my journey toward success. I will forever be indebted to you for instilling perseverance and determination in me.

To So Many More: I cannot begin to thank all those involved with my transformation enough, such as friends, mentors, colleagues, and supporters - you all made this journey possible with your belief and support of my capabilities; they gave me courage and motivation to strive harder in my endeavors and be better. Thank you all so very much.

Your presence has been an incredible gift and I feel empowered by it to pay it forward by helping others achieve greatness. Your collective impact on my life cannot be measured; your influence reverberates through every decision I make and step I take. Thank you, dear ones.

Conclusion

To all who have touched my life and inspired me to pursue greatness, thank you from the bottom of my heart. Thank you for everything you've taught me about how success is not accomplished alone but involves working alongside those around us toward that common goal of greatness. Without you all it would have been much harder.

As I continue this path to financial freedom, I carry with me all your advice, encouragement, and support. You have inspired a fire within me which will continue burning brightly toward fulfilling my dreams and helping me realize them all.

With deep appreciation and a heart full of affection, I offer my sincerest thanks and express my sincerest feelings of appreciation to every one of you!

Landon Gomes

Don't miss out!

Visit the website below and you can sign up to receive emails whenever Landon Gomes publishes a new book. There's no charge and no obligation.

https://books2read.com/r/B-A-EJVZ-CRNMC

Connecting independent readers to independent writers.

Also by Landon Gomes

Growth Series

8 Steps Away From Becoming a Millionaire

About the Author

Hello,

I'm Landon Gomes a Kansascitian (Missouri) grew up less fortunate similar to those of my friends. I'm one of many children, mother has six and father has eight. I am a father myself, an avided reader, I like to think i'm a man of good character and reason. My life goal is to influence change on micro and macro levels.

Thanks,

Landon

About the Publisher

Hello,

If the name Landon Gomes seems familiar, then it would be because I am also the author and publisher of this book. This book/series is a collection of books designed to help the average person who needs some guidance and somewhat of accountability (call to action). I do not wish to impact the entire world, but If I can reach out and help one person who might be on a similar journey by offering the right questions with the correct answers, then I've succeeded in my plan.

The next book in the series will be around credit repair because of the growing need for information in that area. I expect book #2 in this series to be complete and published before the beginning of Fall.

Thanks,

Landon

www.ingramcontent.com/pod-product-compliance
Lightning Source LLC
LaVergne TN
LVHW022028200926
848481LV00007B/2588